W9-ATC-398

COUNTERING THE CONSPIRACY TO DESTROY BLACK BOYS
Volume II

by Jawanza Kunjufu

AFRICAN AMERICAN IMAGES
Chicago, Illinois

Cover photo by Fela Kuumba

Cover design by Eugene Winslow

Photo Credits: Glen Morris and William Hall

Copyright 1986 by Jawanza Kunjufu

Fourth Printing

All rights reserved. No part of this book may be reproduced, stored in retrieval systems, or transmitted in any form, by any means, including mechanical, electronic, photocopying, recording or otherwise, without prior written permission of the publisher.

TABLE OF CONTENTS

Preface

It has been four years since the first release of my book *Countering the Conspiracy to Destroy Black Boys*. My sons, Walker and Shikamana, are now fourteen and nine respectively. They still have years before them until they reach manhood. The response to the book has been overwhelming, with eight printings and 40,000 "official" copies in circulation. (I even appreciate all those who were so interested in the book that they couldn't wait to buy their own, so they copied from a friend, since my major desire is to share the information).

Letters have been received from fathers, mothers, teachers, and community activists concerned about the plight of Black boys. While on the travel circuit, I have had mothers cry in my arms sharing with me the joys and pains of parenting a son. Numerous people have told me I wrote about what they've been thinking for years. They acknowledged that the fine details of the "fourth grade syndrome," mothers "raising daughters and loving sons," and "Simba" were ideas needing conceptualization.

I am pleased that over fifteen new cities have adopted a version of the Simba program, founded in the early seventies by Karenga and Baraka, which brings men and boys together to provide skill development, Black culture, and role models, with the objective of going through the "rites of passage." Nathan and Julia Hare have written a book of the same title formalizing this process. Radio and television documentaries have been developed about Black boys intergrating my work into the larger schematic. On one of the New York radio shows, a boy said at the end, "I'm scared. I need someone to help me be a man." There have been numerous conferences about Black men, but unfortunately, in my opinion, less time is allocated to the plight of Black boys. I choose not to ignore Black men, but to allocate more resources in preventative programs for boys than crisis—oftentimes band-aid—solutions for men.

There is no subject that concerns me more than the development of Black boys into manhood. I have over thirty different workshops offered to pre-school, elementary, high school, and college students, parents, teachers, community and church groups. My experience has taught me that parents bring the greatest level of concern and emotion to the topic. I enjoy more working with a group where apathy and indifference are non-existent and what remains are identifying problem-solving techniques. My greatest challenge comes from those staff members who really don't care if Black boys grow into manhood. To that group I offer this observation: America spends 2,300 dollars per child to attend Headstart and approximately 38,000 dollars per inmate to "attend" prison. The Reagan administration chose to cut Headstart, a program that has shown it is cost effective, and increases expenditures to prisons which have an atrocious record of rehabilitation. Monies spent in Headstart for two years are far less than the lifetime allocations for prison. The auto-mechanic commercial is appropriate for the American taxpayer— "pay me now or pay me later."

Volume II is an answer to the numerous mothers, female teachers, and male community activists who have expressed the need for more information. In every instance, I have asked the parents and teachers to expand their questions and comments. I believe much that we need to know about Black boys lies within fathers, mothers, teachers, and the larger community. For this reason there will be few if any book references. I agreed with my editor, Eugene Winslow, that the solutions for Black boys may not be in books and studies, but in the minds of the numerous people who work with and love our boys on a daily basis. This book is based on all of those conversations we've had together.

In my previous book, *Developing Positive Self Images and Discipline in Black Children*, I shared research from the University of Michigan on factors influencing children.

1950		1980	
1)	home	1)	home
2)	school	2)	peers
3)	church	3)	television
4)	peers	4)	School
5)	television	5)	church

As I previously stated in *Conspiracy,* Vol. I, do not wish to ignore Black girls and women, nor start a debate over who is most oppressed. We *both* are oppressed. I am very concerned with the present trend of literature and film, that portrays Black men as *the* problem and Black females courageously trying to overcome racism, sexism, and Black male oppression single handedly. When one of every two husbands abuse their wives, the problem lies not only with him, but with her.

My "Donna - Kathy" theory, postulates that men are not going to respect women until they first respect themselves. Secondly, men know who to beat and who not to. And lastly, Donna's self-esteem is not predicated on having a man. It's a preference, but it does not determine her self-worth. On the other hand, Kathy will do anything to keep a man, including lowering her self-esteem and becoming irresponsible.

When I address the issue of Black male irresponsibility, it does not exempt the female irresponsibility of having sex before marriage, not using contraceptives, being sexually involved with someone who is not prepared for parenthood, and depending on welfare for financial support. Rather I intend to highlight one of the strategies to destroy the Black family, which is to destroy Black boys before they become men.

Volume II will look at the impact home and school can have on our boys in more detail. The five chapters include "Developing Responsibility in Black Boys," "Female Teachers and Black Male Culture," "Some Reasons Why Black Boys Succeed or Fail," "A Relevant Curriculum for Black Boys," and "Simba" (Young Lion).

Special thanks is given to Eugene Winslow and Sanyika Anwisye for their editing. I thank God for telling me to quit reading for a week, and to write these thoughts. The writing was so inspired, and there were times when my hand was moving so fast, that I knew I was not in control. To God be the Glory.

Many men still believe domestic activities are feminine.

Chapter I

Developing Responsibility in Black Boys

The most frequent response I received upon releasing *Countering the Conspiracy to Destroy Black Boys*, was that more should have been written about the relationship between mothers and sons. The revised edition declared, "some mothers raise their daughters and love their sons." This referred to the practice of some parents, particularly mothers, requiring little of their boys in the areas of household chores and academic excellence. Admittedly, both our boys and girls have problems, but because more responsibility in these areas is often required of girls, it creates the stereotype that household chores and academics are only for girls. Further, it helps to create conflicting expectations in adult male-female relationships: she has learned from her parents to be responsible in those areas and expects him to be also; he hasn't learned, and in addition, expects her to do all the cooking, cleaning, washing, ironing, homework with the children, etc.

The relationship between boys and their mothers is filled with the history of the African-American experience. Presently, mothers can be found positively describing "their little man of the house" or negatively chastening their son by saying, "You're just like your no-good father." My concern in my latest book, *Motivating and Preparing Black Youth to Work*, was parents being annoyed at their children for not possessing drive and enthusiasm despite being given everything. Parents who give everything, and mothers who allow their sons to live at home indefinitely do not help their children grow up. There are mothers who buy their sons expensive gym shoes, stereos, and leather bags, and offer them free room and board with their favorite dessert indefinitely.

I asked mothers in my workshops what are some of the reasons why some "raise their daughters and love their sons." Listed below are their responses and my comments.

1) **The father did not encourage domestic responsibility in the son.**

If the reason why mothers demand less responsibility from their son is because the father doesn't encourage it, this applies to less than 50 percent of the households where the men still reside with their children. I understand mother's concern, because parenting is much more effective when there is mutual agreement.

2) **Mothers lack knowledge of masculinity**

Many men still believe domestic activities are feminine and may lead to homosexuality. A single parent once told me her son did not want to wash dishes the previous night after dinner because it was feminine. The next evening, the parent was going to serve her son on the same dirty plate used previously. The son washed his plate, not because it was masculine or bordering on femininity, but because he wanted his food on a clean plate.

3) **Substitute son to replace the loss or absence of a husband.**

How many mothers view their two-year-old son as someone's future husband or father? How many mothers have come to rely on their strong son to do the physical things around the house that their husband used to do? While I am in favor of boys doing whatever work is necessary, I am concerned about the conscious and often unconscious attempt to keep these forty-year-old sons dependent on them.

4) **Overcompensating for their daughters.**

The concern here lies in the fact that in some households there are double standards, which is not healthy for boys' development and is disastrous for future adult male-female relationships. When daughters are taught to cook, sew, clean, visit libraries and attend church, and are expected to be on the honor roll, while boys are allowed to play basketball all evening after school, never visit libraries or church, cannot boil a hot dog, and have never seen an honor roll, the Black family has a very serious problem.

5) **Protection from racist society.**

This was the historical reason why many mothers shielded their sons, i.e., to keep them from being lynched. This is very complex historically and contemporarily. I don't know if the present-day

The person most likely to teach Black boys to be responsible are Black mothers.

mother consciously thinks about lynching when she lowers her expectation of her son, and does not push him to the apex of society's limit; nor when she overcompensates her efforts for her daughter to reach her full potential.

The question then becomes, who is going to teach Black boys to be responsible in White America? Black men? Female teachers? Ministers? Their peer group? Television? Radio? Their boss? The extended family? Their coach? Father? Mother? I believe the motive for the conspiracy is White male supremacy, but as Alice Walker has commented, "if you think the only reason for our problem is because of somebody else, you have given them a compliment they do not fully deserve." You can blame White men for a portion of the problem, but White men do not determine if our boys wash dishes and clean up their rooms. I can be critical of Black mothers only to a degree, because, unfortunately, the person most likely to teach Black boys to be responsible are Black mothers. This is a major indictment of Black men, specifically Black fathers, many of whom begin their jaunt toward irresponsibility by making a baby they choose not to care for.

I had the honor of speaking at an annual men's conference in Baltimore where the previous year's proceedings declared that the number-one problem facing Black men was economics. I fully understand the dynamics of living in a patriarchal society where men define their role as the family provider, consequently, if unable to provide, self-esteem becomes shattered and staying is a constant reminder of "failure." Studies show that for every 1 percent increase in unemployment there is a 4.3 percent increase in wife abuse, and a 2 percent increase in female headed households. Elliot Liebow's *Tally's Corner* remains a classic describing this plight. The questions I asked at the conference were, "Am I a man today because I have a job, and not a man tomorrow when I don't? Does Black masculinity depend upon Roosevelt's New Deal, Johnson's Great Society, the Humphrey-Hawkins bill, or Reagan's Voo Doo economics?" If so, there will always be a crisis facing Black men, because we have allowed other people to determine whether we are worthy to be called men, and whether or not we should stay with our families.

I have observed different responses from unemployed fathers. Some fathers cry in their misery and make the matter worse with abuse, neglect, and crime; while other fathers under the same circumstance will sell papers or peanuts, or provide landscaping or garbage removal service. Should Black men and women accept these narrow gender roles, or understand that, even while unemployed, they can help their children with homework, teach them the beauty of being unashamedly Black, unapologetically Christian, and assist their wives with housework? Until we redefine manhood and limit the psychological effect of welfare, we will continue to observe boys making babies.

What is being responsible? Webster defines it as accepting obligation, being answerable and accountable. Why are some Black men so irresponsible? I am reminded of a situation where we used to operate a co-op, and would purchase the food from a large distribution facility at 3:00 in the morning. I was a weekly regular, and we had rotating assistants. One brother in particular was always late or absent. As I pondered his circumstances, I observed a chaotic family and an unpredictable lifestyle; he simply did not have the internal fabric to be responsible and consistent. It was often hard for me to accept this because my father worked evenings, but called the house exactly at 8:00 p.m. every night of my childhood. I thought all men were like my father. I now understand that responsibility must be taught early. I am tired of Black women complaining about Black men being irresponsible when they have the best opportunity to correct the problem with their sons. I repeat, *you cannot have an irresponsible man, if he was not also allowed to be irresponsible as a boy.* It is true that our little boys are someone's future husband and father.

Listed below are a list of responsibilities:

personal hygiene	toys equipment
clothes	schedule
room	sexual activity
household chores	residency
siblings	health
allowance	race
studies	God

Who is going to teach Black boys good hygiene and proper grooming? Who is going to insure that Black boys will not play in their better clothes, and will hang them up after school? When will Black boys be expected to make up their beds daily, and clean their rooms periodically? Who has the strength to prevent the possibility of homosexuality and see that your son will wash dishes, mop, vacuum, dust, sew, and cook? When will Black boys be expected to take care of their siblings in preparation for the child-caring of fatherhood? Who will teach their sons how to manage their allowance, so that they won't be like so many men who carry a "wad" of money in their pocket, and cannot explain its whereabouts at the end of the week or month? In our house, both boys are required to save a portion each week; at the end of the year they have an option of spending it and/or saving a portion which we will match and invest. Two lessons are taught; first, what they save each week is very small and could buy very little, but if saved each week for the duration of the year, amounts to a significant sum and promotes the value of saving. Secondly, by offering a matching grant incentive and investment, it teaches them how money can work for them.

Who is going to teach Black boys to do their homework as soon as they come in from school with the music and television off? Who is going to teach them to be responsible for their actions in school, and for their grades? When are Black boys going to learn to take one toy outside at a time, and always bring it back in before bringing out another? When are they going to be taught to put their toys in one location in their room, and how to avoid breaking them? Who is going to teach their sons to respect protocols at activities, and to be punctual about time commitments and class schedules?

Who is going to teach Black boys to do their homework as soon as they come home from school?

When are Black boys going to be responsible for their sexual promiscuity? A documentary titled "The Vanishing Black Family" portrayed a brother who was so irresponsible, many people thought he was an actor. He stated, "Making babies is like a piece of art; you lay back and look at your work." There are parents who know their son has impregnated a sister on the block, but do not hold him accountable. In the same documentary the sisters said, "I want the baby because I want someone to love me, but I don't want to marry the father because he can't even take care of himself." Our society, and specifically families, have a double standard on this issue. Statements such as "boys will be boys, all boys have some dog in them," and "boys have to sow a few wild oats," all reinforce to boys that they can do whatever they feel sexually.

Ninety percent of all teenage pregnancy programs service females. When you hear the phrase *teenage pregnancy*, most people think *girls.* My studies still confirm that it takes consenting parties of both genders to produce a baby. I applaud programs like Project Alpha, Urban League, and Teen Fathers in Cleveland for providing concrete programs and counseling for the "other party." While we need to commend these and other programs holding Black boys accountable, the first level of responsibility still resides in the home. When are parents going to hold their son accountable for his sexual behavior? I believe there is a direct correlation between a boy being allowed to be irresponsible about his hygiene, clothes, room, household chores, siblings, money, studies, toys, activities, schedule, and his sex life. If a boy has been irresponsible about everything else, why should we expect anything different about sex? Another book is needed to explain why girls are also sexually irresponsible. Most adults are not comfortable talking to their children about sex, and especially mothers with their sons. Unfortunately, most boys learn inaccurate sexual information on the streets. Parents often timidly drop a book on their sons bed at sixteen and run out the room saying, "Let me know if you have any questions." Or you get the "open minded" parents who accept that "boys will be boys" or, as the brother in the documentary stated, "I am highly sexed," and give their sons an unlimited supply of condoms.

Research shows that most youths, specifically "high risk" children become sexually active at twelve or thirteen years of age. This is important, because most homes, schools, and churches provide counseling for youth sixteen years and older. The fundamental question is, what is the objective of our counseling? Moral guidance? Contraceptive dispensatory? Many parents and institutions have dropped the first line of defense which is moral responsibility. The second step becomes accepting the act, but protecting yourself against pregnancy. I often tease my workshop audience on teenage pregnancy by declaring, "I can stop teenage pregnancy, if you can stop teenage sex!" Our sad state of affairs is the result of dropping moral responsibility, inadequately preparing our children on the use of contraceptives, and not holding them accountable for their "piece of art." I'm reminded of my father who told me, "If you make it, you will take care of it." I believed him. I actually thought that if a girl's parents came to my house and convinced my parents I was the father of her child, my school plans and savings would have been altered. This kind of background makes a boy think twice about his actions. My father also said, "Welfare didn't make it, and welfare will not take care of it."

The next area of responsibility is the law. Schools and the larger society operate on rules; if they are broken there are direct consequences. Some homes also operate on rules with direct consequences, but when there are no rules at home or no repercussions, the inconsistency is difficult for all youth to understand, especially Black boys who spend a disproportionate amount of time on the streets. Discipline is the number-one problem in elementary schools, and many teachers say, "How can I discipline them when their parents can't or don't?" Who is going to teach Black boys to respect rules, the law, and authority? Again, I refer to my father who told me early on, "If you get caught breaking the law and get locked up, don't even think about calling." I knew my mother would get me out, whatever the reason. Please note, I am very much aware of police brutality and the large number of brothers who are in jail for no other reason than racism and lack of money. I am referring to those unquestionable violations such as rape, burgulary, and murder, where parents can be heard pleading in defense of their son.

Who is going to hold Black boys accountable for becoming employed? People have told me their parents said, "You will either go to school or get a job, but you are not going to lay up in this house." The institutional racism in America confirms Sidney Wilhelm's prediction in his book *Who Needs the Negro*. Alvin Toffler, in the *Third Wave* describes the White power brokers disdain and disregard for Black labor. White suburbia has help-wanted signs in numerous fast food franchises, but many of the jobs are simply inaccessible to Black teenagers, and their minimum wage is not adequate for heads of households. I mentioned earlier that despite the above conditions, some brothers will sell newspapers or peanuts before selling drugs or "pimping" off their mother or "lady." I remember when I could not find work in high school, I volunteered with an electrical firm to learn how to be an electrician. They first questioned my desire to volunteer, then felt sorry for me and gave me bus money, and eventually a little spending money. But more importantly, I learned the basics of being an electrician.

Who is going to teach Black boys to be responsible for their education, employment, and their overall skill development? If Black boys are allowed to stay with their parents indefinitely without contributing financially to the household, and not attending school or developing skill activities, how will they ever learn responsibility? The relationship some boys have with their mothers parallels the parasitic relationships some sisters have with welfare. Each expects nothing from the dependent, consequently the person becomes more irresponsible and dependent.

When are Black boys going to learn the relationship between diet and health? Who is going to prevent our boys from smoking cigaretts at eleven, creating a lifetime addiction and potentially premature death? Life expectancy tables show the following:

European women	77 years
African-American women	75 years
European men	71 years
African American men	64.8 years[1]

Black men often die before the first social security check. Who is going to take Black boys for their annual medical and dental checkup?

Lastly, who is going to teach Black boys to be committed to the liberation of Black people, and to place God first in their lives? In my experience providing cultural and religious programs for youth, I observe different standards for sons and daughters. Why should we be surprised when we see more women involved in cultural and religious activities when, as children, the pattern was already being molded? Many parents require their daughters to attend Black and religious events, but leave it optional for their "little man of the house."

In conclusion, developing responsibility in Black boys is essential if we want the same from Black men. Responsibility starts early, as previously described. The relationship between some mothers and sons not only needs an honest assessment, but it also has implications not only for male-female relations, but also for the association boys have with their female teachers. Often boys think the way they negotiate, plead, rap and manipulate their mothers can also be used with their female teachers, girlfriends, and later, their wives. We have briefly reviewed what some boys encounter at home, particularly from their mothers. The next chapter will look at the relationship between female teachers and the Black male culture.

When a Black boy looks at the female teacher with a look of defiance, I call this "the showdown."

Chapter II

Female Teachers and Black Male Culture

An important factor determining the future of Black boys is predicated on female teachers, especially White teachers. Since *Brown vs. Topeka* of 1954, desegregation has brought more Black boys than ever in contact with White females. The increase in the cost of living has forced many men to leave the educational profession. Recently, with schools unable to provide salaries equivalent to the private sector, and the increase in female-headed households, large numbers of women are pursuing other careers. In the meantime, Black boys are left to be taught by whomever remains, whether they remain voluntarily or because they lack skill, or are too apathetic to advance. Eighty three percent of all elementary teachers are female.[1] Black children constitute 17 percent of all students, but comprise 41 percent of all Special Education placements, primarily Educable Mentally Retarded (EMR), and Behavioral Disorder (BD). Black boys disproportionately are 85 percent of the Black figure. African-American males lead the nation in suspensions.[2]

There are numerous questions that need to be raised. Why are Black children labeled EMR and BD disproportionately? Why are Black boys labeled EMR and BD more than girls? Is there any relationship between female teachers and Black boys being placed in EMR and BD and/or suspended? What are the differences between Black and White female teachers, as it impacts on Black boys? Are there differences between male and female teachers as they relate to the Black male child?

In most school situations, research, marriage, and in everyday life, people look for someone to blame. Often, the victims receive the blame because they have the least resources to defend themselves. Black people are blamed for our plight, yet we are the only group that did not voluntarily come to America looking for a better life. It has been said that the key to the golden rule is: whoever has the gold also has the rule. Therefore, if you must blame someone for a problem, why not blame the victim. Fortunately, scholars like Ryan in "Blame the Victim," and others realize the blame may lie with the perpetrator. It is not my desire to blame either Black boys or female teachers. This would be just as useless as teachers blaming parents and parents blaming teachers, while in the meantime, children suffer. My concern is based on the realistic profile that Black boys will probably attend elementary school for nine years (K-8) and may encounter a maximum of two male teachers—possibly none. And if they are available, it will be in the upper grades, beyond the fourth-grade failure syndrome cited in Volume I.

My purpose is not to blame Black boys or female teachers, but to accept the fact that the educational future of these boys is based on mutual understanding and respect. I do feel presently that schools have placed the burden of blame on boys for their lack of achievement. Even the National (NCAA) rule 48 places the major responsibility on the "athlete-student," to achieve a 2.0 grade point average, and either 15 or 700 on the ACT or SAT respectively. Conversely, elementary and high schools still operate with "social promotion," and every other hinderance to academic success.

Let's first look at female teachers. I believe that how women feel about themselves and the men in their lives is a major factor in their pedagogy. How women feel about their father, boyfriend, husband—or the lack of—is significant. If women have been abused, either in childhood or marriage, and/or have been raped, these are salient issues. In the broad range between "a traditional wife and a lesbian" lies our female teaching corps. On the issues of sexism, plays like *For Colored Girls Only*, and books and movies such as *The Color Purple*, will have an impact on teacher attitudes. Do you really believe that how female teachers feel about themselves, men, and sexism could be left at home and not enter the classroom? What structure exists for female teachers to unload these complicated feelings, or even to determine if they are affecting their male students? What college education department equips female students to isolate these variables for consideration?

For White women it becomes very complex because their Black students may be the first Black males with whom they have ever had direct contact. The above amazes me in its probability. Can you imagine teaching a group of children you have never had meaningful contact with? How can you teach a child whom you do not understand?

Unfortunately, in an insecure world, most people equate differences with inferiority. Black people are different from Whites, and insecure Whites will use this as evidence of White superiority. My position is that Black boys are different from White boys and Black and White girls, but not better or worse. All teachers must develop strategies to maximize Black boys potential.

Now lets look at Black culture, male culture, and its synthesis, Black male culture. It is a sad commentary, but many Blacks do not feel they have a culture. I have not only been told that by Black adults, but also witnessed it in the actions of children. A friend of mine shared with me that a teacher of an international class of children requested that they bring an ethnic dish and wear their cultural dress. The Chinese, Mexican, and German students knew what to bring and wear, but the two Black students brought hamburgers and french fries and wore blue jeans and tee-shirts. I could not fault the students because they only expressed the lack of cultural awareness of their parents. W.E.B. Du Bois in the *Souls of Black Folks*, describes eloquently the "double consciousness and warring souls"—one African, the other American—and the difficulty trying to be African (Black) in White America or how to be American (White) in the Black community. Many Blacks give up trying to please either soul, attempt to become very individualistic, and can be found saying "I am just trying to be me."

Before I share those parts of our culture on which most Blacks of diverse political persuasions agree, let me defend the culture that I am proud of, and explain how I, as a Black parent of the two above mentioned Black students, would have responded had it not been for chattel and mental slavery. I would have dressed my son in a dashiki and my daughter in a buba with her hair wrapped in a gale or profiling cornrows, not French braids or the Bo-Derek look. They would have brought mangoes, avocadoes, plantain, watermelon, millet, okra, blackeye peas and curry chicken. Their notebooks would have pyramid designs and hieroglyphics on them because they would know Egypt is in Africa, not the Middle East; and that Egyptians, not Greeks and Romans, built the first civilization. When the other children chose to speak their native language so that they wouldn't know what they are saying, my children would say "habari gani" in Swahili, which means, "Whats the news?" Lastly, when you have the next international festival, try not to have it on January 15, May 19, August 17, or December 26 through January 1 (those are holy days honoring Dr. King, Malcom X, Marcus Garvey, and Kwanzaa respectively) because my children won't be there. Finally, I would like to have my red, black, and green flag in their class.

While all Blacks cannot agree on the above, our basic cultural elements include:

Language	- Black English, "rappin," slang, oral versus written
Music	- Soul, blues, jazz, gospel, rhythm
Food	- "Soul food," spicy, pork, plentiful
Dress	- Bright colors, flashy design
Religion	- Minister-congregation - call chant response, high percentage of community involvement
Appearance	- Skin color, hair texture, facial features
Learning style	- right brain, relational, people oriented

I often hear terms like "culturally disadvantaged" or "culturally deprived," "dominant culture" or "sub-culture." These are arrogant terms because everyone has a culture, including a people with two warring souls. Culture is lifestyle; it represents the what and how of everything you do.

In my attempt not to blame anyone, but to show mutual responsibility, we cannot afford to have teachers placing negative value judgments on Black culture. When a five-year-old Black child enters kindergarten speaking the language of his or her environment, which may happen to be Black English, this child's self esteem should not have to withstand teacher condemnation. I am not in favor of our children speaking Black English, but the self esteem of the child should not be harmed, when the transfer is made from Black to Standard English. I mentioned earlier that we have White female teachers who are interacting with Black students for the first time. The point I wish to highlight is this also means it is the first time they have experienced Black English, rappin, slang, soul, blues, jazz, rhythm, dress, food, Black standards of beauty, and holistic learning styles. I do not believe you can teach a child you do not understand or respect. Black, Hispanic, and White children are culturally different, but not culturally disadvantaged, unless the definer is culturally arrogant.

Let's now look at male culture which, with the "reported increase" in homosexuality, becomes just as difficult to categorize.

ego - larger and more sensitive than most girls
aggressive

macho - prefers handling problems physically versus
emotionally
athletic - values greater than academic pursuits
non-communicative - less emotional, accent on being
"cool"
risks - peer group uses this as their rites of passage
How many college education departments offer courses on
understanding male culture? I am not suggesting that a course is not
also needed for female culture, but I am advocating that, with a country possessing a disprortionate number of female teachers and a
large number of boys doing poorly, this course may be essential.
Those teachers—Black, White, male, female—who understand and
respect male culture, almost all informed me, learned from their
childhood. The issue of male culture transcends race: White and
Hispanic boys display similar characteristics. In my opinion, all three
groups are known for their ego, aggression, athletic orientation, non-
communication, and taking risks. These groups differ primarily in
degrees; Hispanic males are more aggressive and macho than the
other two, Black males are more athletic, and White males have
larger egos.

Where the members of the three groups end up depends more
on institutional racism than teachers understanding their culture.
Hispanic males possess the highest dropout rate, which is attributed
to the language barrier and the strict gender roles of being the provider regardless of the age. Black males disproportionately lead in
EMR, suspension, and athletic scholarships. (The latter will be cur-
tailed with NCAA rule 48, which I am only in favor of if equal pressure
is placed on elementary and high schools). White males also suffer
from a female-run classroom, but when placed in special education
rather than EMR, will be classified learning disabled (LD), where
more learning is required. White males need only finish high school to
exceed the income levels of all other groups with college degrees. My
concern remains for Black and Hispanic males who are not as fortunate. That's why Lerone Bennett says "the question of education
for Black people in America is a question of life and death. It is a
political question, a question of power. Struggle is a form of education, perhaps the highest form."[3]

Let's now combine the Black culture of language, music, food,
dress, religion, appearance, and learning style with the male culture,
which consists of ego, aggression, athletics, non-communication,
and risk orientation. The synthesis should give a reasonable view of

Black male culture. Black male culture encompasses all the characteristics of male culture and everything from Black culture except religion. Large numbers of Black boys think the church is for women and sissies. Those that attend primarily worship because it's required. Reasons for this sentiment include a passive, pie-in-the-sky approach to contemporary problems and a white image of Jesus Christ. I have noticed across the country, those churches—Christian or Islamic, including my own—that have political and cultural programs and activities have larger numbers of men and youth.

Expressions of this synthesis are "the rap," "dozens" (signifyin), "the walk," the leaning of the head with a hat, and a tremendous regard for the peer group. (Other classroom characteristics will be provided in chapter four on curriculum). Female teachers must understand that Black boys value their peers, walk, hat, "rap" and signifyin more than anything else. Teachers are not going to sway these boys to their way of thinking with a condemnation of things they value. Many female teachers do not even know how much Black boys value these, and some have told me they did not know what were the "dozens." College education departments don't teach the importance of these, consequently the only way to know would be to have lived or observed this culture; but there are even Black teachers and male teachers who grew up in it, and express their disdain and condescension for it. Please do not think that mere condemnation saps boys' desire to continue valuing these cultural expressions.

I am not condoning the dozens, nor any other facet of Black male culture, but if we want to save Black boys, we must transfer their cultural strengths into the classroom experience. This chapter is designed to familiarize teachers with Black male culture. The last chapter will attempt to show how these cultural patterns can be integrated into the curriculum to maximize student achievement. A teacher who understands and is sensitive to the male ego and peer group acceptance would take this into consideration when making public admonishments. If there is one characteristic that is the most misunderstood and causes Black boys to be suspended or placed in EMR and BD, it's the "dozens."

The dozens is an activity primarily performed by males, in which usually two opponents dual verbally. They make derogatory comments about each other and each other's family members, usually the mother. The performance of each player is appreciated and judged by the group who urges them on. This is called a manhood rite, because it serves an important function. The boy must master several

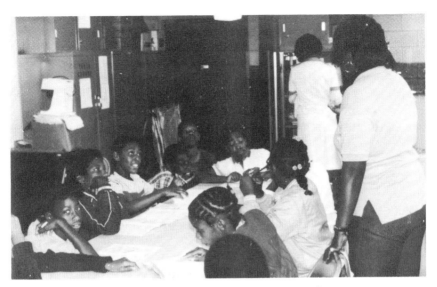

When Black male children volley verbally in an aggressive manner, some teachers don't understand.

important competencies in order to be a good player. First of all, he must control his emotions. Here in the presence of his friends, terribly derogatory statements are made about his mother, who is dear to him. He must suppress his emotional reaction to what has been said, so that he can think quickly and counter with an even more clever slur upon his opponent's mother. Unfortunately, when Black male children volley verbally in an aggressive, threatening manner, some teachers don't understand it, and interpret their behavior as fighting, when actually they were "signifyin" to relieve tension and avoid a fight. Large numbers of Black males are labeled disciplinary problems, EMR, and suspended because of the "dozens" or "signifyin." People not understanding Black culture take words literally and to heart. When Black parents tell their children, "I'm going to knock you into the middle of next week," the phrase needs to be tempered with a Black culture perspective.

An important component of both Black and Black male culture is the oral tradition. Historically, it was the griot, the elder of the community who passed along the information to its members. Principals express disappointment to me when they send home hundreds of PTA announcements and only a few parents are in attendance. My experience has been that Headstart and those schools with a parent coordinator, staff, and principal willing to personally extend an invitation, either direct or by telephone, receive a far greater response. For Black boys, the ability to rap (words strung together in rhyme) with the objective to influence a girlfriend, mother, and, if possible, the teacher, and signify is valued by a people with a strong oral tradition. The following chapter will include how the walk, leaning head, and hat affect the learning process.

Exampled below are two students who often receive a different classroom experience, yet sit next to each other.

Ten-year-old Renee has light skin, with "good" hair, "keen" features, and "pretty" eyes. She wears nice lace dresses with a ribbon in her hair daily. She is slightly shy, but has a radiant smile that she flashes when complimented.

Willie is also ten, but is big for his age. He has dark skin, short "nappy" hair, and "broad" features. Willie wears the same jeans to school for a week, but only wears the top twice. He talks loud and shows off in front of his friends, and in this picture has his arms crossed looking defiant. Are your expectations the same for both students? What do you feel when a ten-year old Black boy folds his arms and looks you directly in the eye?

When a Black boy looks at the female teacher with a look of defiance, I call this the "showdown" between female teachers and Black boys. If the "dozens" did not exclude them from the mainstream, in most instances it will be the showdown. Black boys could avoid this confrontation if they looked and acted like Renee. Black male culture unfortunately is not always interested in being cooperative, quiet, and dainty. Female teachers could avoid this exhibition if they would come out of themselves and appreciate Willie for what he represents. In Volume I, a chapter titled the "Fourth Grade Failure Syndrome" documented that Black boy's test scores decline from this point. The concern is, why are we unable to maintain their enthusiasm and achievement levels with each passing year? There are numerous reasons for this decline: less nurturance and movement; less student questions and parental involvement; greater influence by the peer group; more classroom competition; more left-brain, analytical, and task oriented learning; few male teachers; and finally, they are becoming as big as the teacher, so size is no longer a factor. Whatever strategies based on teachers being larger that may have been used in the primary grades, will not work in the intermediate and upper grades.

The showdown will not always match strength against strength. Some female teachers are *afraid* of Black boys. I do not believe you can teach a child while afraid. This may be the reason why only 45 percent of all secondary teachers are women. Male teachers can be found in the high schools, and possibly in upper elementary grades. The problem is we are losing large numbers of Black boys before they reach grades eight through twelve. I have also observed a very strong, effective teaching staff in alternative schools, GED, and adult education. Principals continue to tell me they must place their stronger teachers in the upper grades. This is a band-aid approach. How effective is this strategy, when we are losing students before they encounter these "relief teachers"?

When a Black boy looks at the female teacher with a look of defiance, many factors previously mentioned are at stake. How do female teachers feel about themsleves? How do they feel about men? Where are they on the continuum between "traditional" wife and "lesbian"? What has been their exposure to Black culture? Do they understand our society is partriarchal? When they see Willie, do they see a future Jesse Jackson or a drug addict?

What is going on inside the Black boy? Is he trying to show off in front of his friends? Is this one of the risks required for the rites of passage? Has he decided that discipline is associated with physical force, i.e., the belt, and feels confident now that he is bigger, and strength and size are now in his favor? Does he really want to be taught, loved, understood, and given some direction? Is he challenging any adult to determine if there is anyone capable?

The showdown begins; listed below are some of the potential outcomes.

(1) Female teachers out of emotional control hollers at the child, class laughs, Willie sits down slowly, causing further lesson disruption. The class, Willie, and probably the teacher knows Willie won this battle.

(2) Female teacher responds inconsistently to Willie's behavior. He wins all those actions that are ignored, and if her response was unassertive, he also wins.

(3) Female teacher sends Willie downstairs to the principal's office; probable actions include suspension, EMR placement, and eventually expulsion. Willie wins against the female teacher; he may lose to the principal, or special education teacher, but not to her.

(4) Female teacher sends Willie to the corner or outside the classroom door. This showdown is a draw; the battle has been delayed indefinitely.

(5) Female teacher assertively and consistently tells Willie to go to his seat and he complies. Female teacher wins all encounters.

(6) A Chicago public school teacher shared this final showdown. She began teaching a "slow group" of eighth-grade students, starting in mid-year. One of the male students, identical in every facet to Willie (she had been previously warned that no one could handle Willie) began staring at her. Whenever and wherever she moved, he kept staring at her. He would look at her, and she would look at him, then he would smile. Willie's objective without his arms folded was to make her uncomfortable. He was going to rule the class just by a strong look in his eye. The teacher told me she returned every look and smile, and at the end of the day, they both quietly had mutual respect for each other. Teacher wins.

The showdown is a battle of strength, and adults cannot win without "leverage". Many homes use the belt as this source. A major problem for schools results when children only respect physical punishment, and not also assertive communication, behavior modification, and denials. Coaches are effective because they use uniforms, letters, game participation, trophies, scholarships, and potential stardom as their source of leverage. Teachers possibly can use grades, but this is ineffective if not reinforced in the home, and if the students do not see their future place in the society. Please remember there is a direct relationship between schools and the economy. The acceptance of standardized English is greatly affected by the employment outlook. This is consistent with the golden rule theory. Most people speak the language of their employers. This may explain the continued use of Black English with a sixty percent Black teenage unemployment rate and higher for Black males. The only other leverage a teacher—black, white, male, or female—has when you exclude the belt, NBA, grades, and jobs, is the combination of love, cultural understanding, and mutual respect.

We have now looked in more detail at the role mothers and female teachers play in our boys development. In spite of the above, some boys are able to avoid the conspiracy. If we can understand why in chapter three, we may be able to help other boys less successful.

Chapter III

Some Reasons Black Boys Succeed or Fail

(Following are some case studies which are not real, but the reasons for success are based on actual experiences.)

Case Study I

Ron Gilliam is entering his fourth year of college, and has hopes of being drafted as a running back by the pros. Ron has won numerous awards as an athlete, dating back to his middle-school playing days. I asked him how he was able to stay in school when so many of his friends either dropped or were pushed out. Ron said, "I liked playing ball, and there was more competition playing school ball than sandlot and park district. I didn't like school very much, but looked forward to 3:15 when practice started. They held me back a year in elementary school, but I knew they couldn't hold me a second year because I would be fifteen years old. Some of my friends said I was a better ball player than everybody else in middle school because I was older and bigger. I was determined to show them in high school, where the upperclassmen were larger and older, that I was good.

Sometimes the high school coach would watch the middle-school teams play. I heard he asked about me and when they expected me to graduate. I knew then I was going to graduate, but maybe not on time. A lot of my friends played ball after school, but it was in the park or around the house. For some reason sports didn't have the same effect on them. Most of them dropped out around their sophomore year because they didn't like the teacher or vice versa. I knew how they felt because they were in remedial classes with the dumb people, and it was embarrassing. I knew I wasn't bright, but I persevered for practice, then I became a star. I knew if I could endure 9:00 till 3:00, I could go to the pros. Playing ball was always easier than diagramming sentences.

"My high school coach only had to talk to my teacher about changing my grades twice. He always felt the best way was to develop my schedule, giving me a light, easy load and going to summer school each year. My college coach used the same procedure. I don't know what I'll do if I don't get drafted. I don't have enough hours to graduate, and hadn't thought about any other career except running back. I feel pretty good. I didn't drop out, I graduated from elementary and high school. I'm in college, and one telephone call away from the NFL."

Case Study II

Lawrence Drew has just graduated from elementary school as the top student in the class. He has big plans for repeating this feat in high school, earning a college scholarship, and becoming a doctor. Lawrence has a strong mother, Cynthia, who runs a tight ship. She is a single parent; she was divorced when he was five years old; Lawrence may see his father once a year. The mother is an accountant, and has been taking courses over the past three years in hopes of becoming a Certified Public Accountant. I had the opportunity to visit them one evening, and asked about Lawrence's success. Cynthia responded, "Nothing but the Lord. I pray constantly, because the streets are so dangerous. Lawrence calls me at work when he gets home from school. He knows to do his homework first; if he does not have any, or not enough for an hour, I bought him workbooks to supplement. He can watch television, but for only two hours each day. We also have one hour for reading a library book of his choice. He writes a paper about the book that is due before he goes rollerskating on Saturday. We read the Bible daily, and attend church regularly."

I asked Lawrence, who is very quiet, if he could explain his success. Lawrence added, "My friends sometimes call me a sissy because I don't play as long as they do, and because I get good grades. I try to get my mom to let me play more basketball and learn martial arts. I think she is becoming more understanding. She is tough, but what can I say? She runs it, and its not that bad being valedictorian."

Case Study III

Jamaal Brock is in eighth grade in a private school. He was labeled a behavioral disorder (BD) in fourth grade at the neighborhood public school. His parents objected at the staffing where the decision was made; and Mrs. Brock, a school teacher, requested that, if he must be placed, she preferred learning disabled. When children are placed in special education, there is a disproportionate number of Whites placed in LD versus Blacks in BD and EMR. The psychologist, principal, and teacher were adamant on Jamaal being placed in BD. The Brocks grudgingly conceded, but decided if there was no improvement they would place him in a small private school the following year. The decision in June was not to mainstream Jamaal back into his regular class, but another year of BD. The Brocks, who were unable to place Jamaal in a private school during the middle of the school year at the time of the staffing, enrolled their son in a highly acclaimed private school in the fall.

Jamaal is an only child, and likes a lot of attention. He has a strong need to be liked by his peers, and is easily influenced. He is a good student when he concentrates and pays attention. Howalton is a small private school with a student-teacher ratio of 20 to 1. The school prides itself on being academically challenging, with a good measure of discipline. Students who act up get a chance to visit Mr. Watson and his paddle before they call their parents to explain what happened. I talked to Jamaal about his new school. Jamaal offered these remarks: "At my old school, I had more fun. We would throw spitballs at the girls until we were sent downstairs. That wasn't so bad, because we missed all our assignments. This school doesn't play. I don't know if the school is so strict or the students are chicken, but I do know what went on at PS 192, doesn't go on here. My report card is okay. I got three C's, three B's, and one A. I miss my old friends, but my parents feel this is a better school. I would like to go to a public high school, but I think my parents will send me to another private school. I don't blame them; I haven't been in Mr. Watson's office since fifth grade, and my report card is better."

Case Study IV

Carl Hampton is graduating from high school tonight. Watching proudly from the audience are his mother, two younger sisters, and his uncle. Tonight may appear easy, but the journey was filled with obstacles. The mother was emotionally and physically abused by her husband, Carl's father. He neglected Carl and his sisters, and officially left home when Carl was at the ripe age of nine, entering the critical fourth grade-failure syndrome. Coincidentally, his uncle Brian, his mother's younger brother was just returning home from college after graduation. Uncle Brian stepped in and had a major impact on Carl's life. A few days after graduation, Brian, Carl, and I had this conversation. I asked Carl and Brian to describe the graduation journey. Carl said, "I was just out there. My parents were breaking up, my mother said I would be the 'man of the house,' and my friends were into ditching school and stealing. My mother had more than she could handle just paying the bills, and 'raising' my sisters."

Brian commented, and while he spoke, Carl's look of admiration told the story. Uncle Brian had a degree in computer programming and design. Carl did not have his first male teacher until eighth grade, consequently, if not for his uncle, he would not have seen a Black male academic role model until then. Brian said, "I love my sister, always have, and anything I could do to help, I always tried. I would take Carl to games, programs, and sometimes let him just hang out with me on Saturday, but only if he had a good week in school. I would represent him at those programs where fathers' attendance is encouraged. I knew my sister was a good person, but she was weak in choosing men and would possibly be the same in 'raising' one."

Case Study V

Robert Wagner, a seventh grader, is a small-to-medium size kid with curly hair who speaks standard English. His favorite subjects are math and science, and he has excellent critical thinking skills. He has a knack for taking tests, but doesn't do as well on his report card. He is slightly hyperactive, but teachers have found this occurs when he's not being stimulated. I had an opportunity to talk to Robert's teacher. I asked Mrs. Pierce how Robert was able to avoid the decline in achievement demonstrated by large numbers of Black boys. She stated, "Robert simply has innate ability. A couple of teachers over the years have suggested special placement for Robert, but how can you rationalize that when he often has the highest scores on achievement tests? Robert is not working at his potential, but that does not warrant special education. Most teachers simply like Robert. He's a loving kid, speaks well, and avoids getting caught like most boys when doing something mischievous."

In presenting the Conspiracy workshop across the country, frequently someone will offer themselves or someone they know to refute the theory. Often, they expand their premise and suggest just as they or someone else "made it," so can all Black boys. In that same spirit, good-intentioned teachers say "if I can just save one."

Carl Boyd, a good friend of mine, counters with, "if I can just *lose* one." Are we willing to accept the figures that at birth there are 1.03 Black boys to 1.0 Black girls, but at eighteen years 1.0 available Black men to 1.8 available Black women? Are we willing to accept the loss of one of every two? What number are you willing to lose? Should we be satisfied that Ron, Lawrence, Jamaal, Carl, and Robert survived the conspiracy? Is there anything we can learn from these case studies, that we can pass on to others less fortunate?

Let's review the factors resulting from the case studies.

Name	Significant Factors
Ron Gilliam	Athlete, coach
Lawrence Drew	Strong family background, religion, middle class values, on a continuum from macho (physical) to sissy (mental) (macho-sissy , skewed toward mental)
Jamaal Brock	Private school, less negative peer pressure, small student-teacher ratio, higher teacher expectations
Carl Hampton	Significant other, excluding parents and coach
Robert Wagner	Innate ability, left-brain thinking, (skills ideal for test taking) speaks standard English, considered physically appealing, and societal survival skills

Conversely, those brothers who do not possess these above variables are at risk. These brothers can be described as follows:

   not on a school athletic team
   non-academic household
   lower economic class, (cannot afford private school)
   non-religious
   macho
   influential peer group
   low teacher-expectations
   no significant role model
   right-brain thinking
   African features
   Black English
   no societal survival skills

How many boys do you know who are not on a team, come from a poorly academic household, are impoverished, do not attend church, are aggressive, hang with a negative peer group, are given

Constructive programs can help Black boys enter manhood.

low teacher-expectations or placed in special education, are in a large classroom, have no advocate, think better relational than abstract, have dark skin with short nappy hair and broad features, speak Black English, and lack western sophistication? These boys are highrisk and prime candidates for not entering manhood. Every effort, program, person, and dollar should be allocated to avoid this tragedy.

In retrospect, please note these are partial solutions to our problem. If we know that placing a boy on a school athletic team may encourage him to graduate, it should be pursued. If we can show parents that they do make a difference, and that monitoring homework and television, and supplementing classwork is significant, it may motivate more parents. If we can show parents that dollars invested in education will bring a greater return than your new car note, clothing accounts, and weekend recreation, it may alter expenditures. If we can show families that "the Lord is able and ask anything that you will in my name," it may increase the number of worshippers. If we steer boys to the center of the continuum between macho and sissy we may be able to redefine manhood.

I would like to address this issue in more detail. I think it is crucial, and in Volume I, an entire chapter on male seasoning looked at the perceptions boys have of manhood. Michael Brown mentioned that "some brothers think it is how much pain you can inflict on another person; how many girls you can impregnate and not get married; how much reefer you can smoke, pills you can drop and wine you can drink; how many times you can go to jail and come out unrehabili- tated; what kind of clothes you wear, how much money you have, and what kind of car you drive."[2]

The chances of boys falling to the right of center (more intellec- tual than physical) is greatly reduced if parents allow unlimited time on the streets, and do not know their son's friends. All peer groups are not negative; Ron Gilliam's peer group is his teammates, and Lawrence Drew's peer group is his church choir and Simba. Parents need to understand the street's peer-group desire to evaluate how well a brother can handle himself either athletically or defensively. Parents make a critical mistake going from one extreme to another by removing their sons from the basketball court to piano, versus half the day in the library or with the piano, and the other half in martial arts or basketball.

If we know the impact that teacher expectations, student-teacher ratios, and special education placements have on children's future, we should visit the classroom at least once, exchange numbers with the teacher, and bring Black professional educators to those staff- ings. If we understand that the reason we are "successful" is not because of some great talent, but because someone took the time to help us develop it, we would reach back and help other family, block, and church members. Uncle Brian saved a Black boy from futility. If teachers understand that Black children, and particularly Black boys, have a culture that encourages a right-brain approach, and would alter their curriculum to utilize this strength; and if parents understood that from the fourth grade on, their culture needs to include a left-brain curriculum which encourages analytical applications, we could possibly arrive at an equillibrium.

If teachers could overcome the value judgements of beauty and feel the same way about dark skin, little Black boys with nappy hair and broad features as they do about Renee who has light skin, long hair, and "pretty" eyes, and wears lace dresses with ribbon in her hair, than Black boys may receive an equal chance. If teachers would not place a value judgment on Black English, and learn how to teach standard English without condeming the child; and if Black parents realized how significant language usage is to student achievement, they may reinforce teacher recommendations.

The last reason that was identified was societal survival skills. Black boys need to be taught from an African frame of reference, the distinction between a battle and a war. I am reminded of the movie "Ragtime," where the star Rollins, made his damaged new car a war rather than a battle. He determined the damaging of his car was worth losing his wife, child, job, and ultimately his life. Do you know how many Black boys lose their lives or their freedom because of how they respond to police? When I was growing up, four of my friends and I were playing ball in an alley. A police car drove down the alley, and two officers asked us if we had seen two teenagers accused of a recent robbery. Four of us answered their questions, but the other decided he "wasn't telling the 'pigs' nothing." The police decided one inconvenience deserved another, and took him to the station until his parents signed for his release.

Many Black boys arrive at this position of militancy without any dialogue with their parents or other respected adults. I began by saying these societal survival skills need to be taught from an African frame of reference. I am not suggesting that we not stand up for what is right, but I am stating we need to determine in a logical manner, how much we are willing to sacrifice. Secondly, standing up for an issue does not negate the importance of *how* you express your views. Thirdly, it concerns me how militant we can be over a car or questions in a alley, but when its time to vote, boycott, buy black products, and volunteer time to the black community, we find very few men standing up. There is a difference between a battle and a war. The same people that criticize Dr. King for being passive, don't realize that the man believed in non-violent *resistance*, and did not back down on his disdain for the Vietnam war. Dr. King died over Vietnam, not over a brother stepping on his shoes or talking to his lady.

This same misconception between battles and wars follows Black boys into the classroom. Black boys choose to make a war out of situations with their classmates, teachers, and principal. In the previous chapter, I made reference to the defiant boy with his arms folded. The boy has decided to take a stand. The teacher said, "Get back to work," and he folds his arms and looks either down or away. He has chosen not to unfold his arms, nor make eye contact. Before teachers reading this book start nodding their heads, the fundamental lesson here is: Black boys have not been taught other ways to express their manhood. This requires men, sensitive female teachers, and parents to find healthier expressions.

I believe we have to give our children, especially Black boys, something to lose. Children make foolish choices when they have nothing to lose. Children think twice about drinking, smoking, stealing, and becoming pregnant when they have something to lose. Boys shoot people for stepping on their shoes when they don't feel good about themselves. These acts really become suicide missions. When boys behave like this in school, indirectly they are expressing a desire to be expelled, because they don't feel good about their achievement. Even the "athlete-student," who doesn't like his classes, understands the difference between a battle and a war. He will not defy a teacher if he feels it may impinge upon his privilege to play. A boy who has self-esteem, identified talents, family or racial pride, teacher or coach expectation, scholarship, career, or faith in God will make sensible choices between battles and wars.

Large numbers of Black boys have been suspended because they refused to say yes or no ma'am or sir, apologize, take off their hats, alter their walk, talk softer, smile, or change their body language. Robert Wagner survived the conspiracy, not because he was quiet in class, but because he found talking softer allowed him not to get caught as frequently. When he did get caught he was smart enough to smile at the teacher, apologize, and get back to work. He did not feel talking to his friend in class was a war. It was a battle he would like to have won, but if he fought the battle and lost, he would not be around for the war. We have lost a lot of brothers in battle; *and in the war to save the Black family, we have very few brothers available.*

The next chapter will attempt to move from theory to practice. I always ask in my conspiracy workshops, "What kind of curriculum and teaching style can we develop to maximize Black boys' potential?" Very few answers have been forthcoming, but several teachers and I brainstormed together and came up with several suggestions.

You cannot teach a child you do not love. You cannot teach a child you do not respect. You cannot teach a child you do not understand.

Chapter IV

A Relevant Curriculum for Black Boys

One of the major reasons why I wrote Volume II, was because I kept asking myself, "What kind of curriculum and pedagogy can we develop to maximize Black boys' potential?" I encourage readers to try to answer the question themselves before reading on, and to inform me of their findings upon completion of this book so that I can share it with the public. I optimistically believe that most teachers would like to reach Black boys rather than place them in Special Education or suspension. I felt if the workshop could be a working session where we all share ideas and successful lesson plans, it would be mutually rewarding. Most formal workshops have not resulted in answering this research question. The reasons for this include the shortage of time, the staff's perception that the consultant is the expert rather than collective brainstorming, and what I've noticed is a subtle, but often an overt resistance to alter their curriculum or style to meet the needs of Black children, and specifically boys.

Unfortunately, there are teachers who teach with the attitude, "I got mine and you get yours." Many teachers teach the way they were taught as children, as college students, or the way they like to learn. They ask, why should I have to change the way I teach for Black boys? In the "Effective Schools Project," Ron Edmonds notes that in schools of low achievement, the most negative room in the school is the teacher's cafeteria. The room will be filled with condescending negative comments about the futility of teaching "these children." Effective schools have a positive learning climate, that does not allow this attitude to permeate its facility.[1]

Piaget says "instructors teach their subjects, but teachers understand how children learn." This further explains the fourth grade syndrome. As children move into the upper grades and high school, less concern is allocated to the student, and more attention is given to the subject matter. High school teachers are the absolute worst. They will quickly inform you, "I am a geometry teacher." They mean that they teach only geometry. Who cares about the fact that the student maybe lacking in self-esteem, motivation, or reading comprehension?

I open all my teacher workshops by declaring "you cannot teach a child who you do not love. You cannot teach a child who you do not respect. You cannot teach a child who you do not understand. You cannot teach a child whom you are afraid of. You cannot teach a child if your 'political baggage' i.e. sexism and racism, is brought into the classroom." (How many teachers do you know who have the ability to keep their past experiences about racism and sexism outside the door?) You cannot teach a child without bonding first, which results from love, respect, and understanding.

When you teach Black boys, what do you see? Earlier I made reference to Jesse Jackson or a drug addict. Whatever you see will be what you produce. Do you have the same expectations for Renee and the defiant Black boy? Research has shown that not only are expectations the major factor in student achievement, but even within the same classroom, teachers have different levels of expectations. The Teacher Expectations Student Achievement (TESA) model is an excellent tool to evaluate consistency. The model is divided into three separate categories for observation.

Response Opportunities	Feedback	Personal Regard
1) Equitable distribution	1) Affirm or correct students performance	1) Proximity
2) Individual helping	2) Praise	2) Courtesy
3) Delving	3) Listening	3) Personal interests
4) Higher level questioning	4) Accepting feelings	4) Touching

Can you honestly say that in each category and to the fourth degree you provide each child the same level of expectations? Studies show that teachers give girls 3.2 seconds to respond to a question versus 2.7 for boys. This figure widens for Black girls and boys and becames progressively wider over the school year.[2]

The research question remains: What kind of curriculum and pedagogy can we develop to maximize Black boys potential? I believe this question has been answered in numerous articles by A. W. Boykin, Henry Morgan, and Na'im Akbar. I feel books by Janice

Hale, Paulo Friere, James Banks, and William Glasser have contributed much to this question. I advocate the best contributions have come from Asa Hilliard, Council of Independent Black Institutions (CIBI), and The Cultural Linguistic Approach (CLA). In my earlier book, *Developing Positive Self Images and Discipline in Black Children*, the above models were reviewed and some of my own were added. Listed below briefly are a few salient features.

Asa Hilliard offers:

The School

As it is in general (Analytical)	As it could be (Relational)
Rules	Freedom
Standardization	Variation
Conformity	Creativity
Memory for specific facts	Memory for essence
Regularity	Novelty
Rigid order	Flexibility
"Normality"	Uniqueness
Differences equal deficits	Sameness equal oppression
Preconceive	Improvise
Precision	Approximate
Logical	Psychological
Egocentric	Global
Convergent	Sociocentric
Controlled	Divergent
Meanings are universal	Expressive
Direct	Meanings are contextual
Cognitive	Indirect
Linear	Affective
Mechanical	Patterned
Unison	Humanistic
Hierarchical	Individual in group
Isolation	Democratic
Deductive	Integration
Scheduled	Inductive
Thing focused	Targets of opportunity
Constant	People focused
Sign oriented	Evolving
Duty	Meaning oriented
	Loyalty[12]

Many psychologists connect this model to the split brain theory. The brain is divided into two apparently symmetrical parts. The left side of the brain is analytical, divides things into sections, and specializes in the functions of math and science. The right hemisphere is more holistic, relational, and appreciates the areas of music, art, dance, and sports. Returning to Piaget's comment about instructors and teachers, do we ignore the strength of Black children on the right side of the brain? Another reason for the fourth-grade failure syndrome is that with each grade level a more left-brain curriculum is implemented. A most graphic illustration are the larger number of college graduates who draw on a primary level. The curriculum of most schools simply ignore most other forms of learning except the written word.

I offer five forms of instruction:

> written
> oral
> pictures
> artifacts
> fine arts

The last four emphasize the right side of the brain. I am not suggesting that we exclude the left hemisphere or analytical learning; that would be just as harmful as the present situation which excludes right-brain, relational learning. I'm advocating all five forms of instruction to enhance that more children grasp the concept. The following examples are offered.

(1) Two students are learning to dance; one with a left brain analytical approach, the other with a right-brain relational approach. The first child goes to a dance studio, and follows the floor chart on when and where to step until he succeeds. The second student goes to a disco and observes for a period of time, then gets on the dance floor, and does his/her "own thing." Which approach was correct?

(2) The teacher announces she will give 100 points in extra credit for additional reading, 75 points for an oral presentation, and 10 points for an illustration. Is this evaluation fair to all learners?

(3) Teachers can either assign students to:
   (a) Read and write the definitions.
   (b) Read the definition and trace the picture.
   (c) Read the definition and create your own image.

Which exercise encompasses both analytical and relational learning?

(4) Children know that 6 × 3 = 18, but in a word problem don't know when to use the multiplication skill.

The above example has several pedagogical and cognitive points that require illumination. The analytical learner who breaks an operation into parts is more comfortable separating a skill from its usage. The relational learner needs to be given the objective before the skill is taught. An increasing number of students, including analytical thinkers, are lacking motivation because they don't see the relevance of the lesson. It concerns me that Black boys are labeled slow learners in the classroom, and yet, on the streets and in the military, understand math and science applications very well.

How can a brother fail math in school, and yet without pencil, paper or calculator, tell each one of his friends what they will pay for a bottle of Wild Irish Rose? Is it because the street curriculum is real, and one mistake could be costly or deadly? Did the motivation to learn come before or after the skill? Military training is another excellent example of blending theory with practice, analytical with relational.

The military gives an overview of its objectives, followed by theoretical readings, and culminating with applied demonstrations on actual equipment. Again, many Black boys that were placed in EMR and suspended do very well in the military. (I am not overlooking institutional racism expressed in the disproportionate number of Black men on the frontline as compared to behind-the-line technicians and officers and their imperialistic objectives). A sound educational theory shows the need first and encourages questions. Another component of the fourth grade failure syndrome is an inverse relationship between age and questions. What is it about our pedagogy that the longer students sit in school the fewer questions they ask and the less motivated they become? A sound theory uses a number of methods to disseminate information, and evaluates it in the same number of methodologies. The military not only informs its students by reading, films, and artifacts, but also evaluates learning in writing, orally, and field demonstrations.

The cultural linguistic approach has developed an entire culture-based educational curriculum in social studies, mathematics, science, and language arts as well as a instructional methodology called USISPU

U - Unstructured Elicitation
S - Structured Elicitation
I - Interim
S - Structured Elicitation
P - Practice
U - Unstructured Elicitation

A sample lesson plan

Concept: All people are alike and different in many ways.

Performance: The child will be able to identify other people who are similar to him in the dimensions of race, sex, and age.

Materials: Pictures—Black ABC's
Filmstrips—*Getting to Know Me*
Books—*Colors Around Me*

Procedure: Motivation—Teacher shows class various pictures of Black children.

U- Tell me everything you can about this picture. (The objective is to use Black children's oral strength and culture heritage to stimulate further cognition).

S- Tell me what color of skin this child has.
Tell me what color the child's eyes are.
Tell me something about the child's hair.

I- Class, these are pictures of Black children. Why do we call them Black children? How many of us think these children look like you?
There are lots of skin colors that little Black children have.

Have them draw a picture of themselves.

S- Tell me what color of skin this child has.
Tell me what color his eyes are.
Tell me something about this child's hair.

P- My name is _____
I am _____ years old.
My eyes are _____
My hair is _____
I belong to the _____ race
I am a _____ (boy/girl)

U- Tell me everything you can about this picture.

So far we have looked at curriculum strategies and teacher styles primarily to benefit Black children and all other children who have a relational orientation. In my workshops I often ask for female teachers only, to answer the question what are some of the differences between boys and girls in the classroom? If we accept Piaget's contention about instructors and teachers, we must determine male classroom characteristics and then create a curriculum that it will complement. The list reflects brainstorming between many teachers and myself.

Male Classroom Characteristics
aggressive
athletic
shorter attention span
slower maturation rate
less cooperative
larger
influenced more by peer group
greater interest in math than reading
gross motor greater than fine motor skills
interested in fine arts
not as neat
louder
prefer hats
distinct walk
larger and more sensitive ego
signifying/dozens/rappin

Many of these characteristics were mentioned in chapter two, where I looked at Black male culture. This consistency further reinforces the need to understand the culture of the child in the learning process. I again want to return to the research question: What kind of curriculum and pedagogy can we develop to maximize Black boys potential? Please review the male classroom characteristics. What curriculum changes or teaching styles should be altered within the context of these factors? I would like to isolate (1) shorter attention span, (2) influenced more by their peer group, (3) greater interest in math than reading, (4) more advanced skills in gross versus fine motor, (5) keen interest in fine arts, (6) larger and more sensitive ego, and lastly (7) playing the dozens.

(1) Shorter attention span.
Large numbers of Black boys are labeled Special Education

because they are "hyperactive." This word is filled with value judgments and complexities. Hyper has to be based on a norm, which in America is white. Psychologists such as Garber, Boykin, and Wilson document the higher vibrancy, capital, and verve that Black children bring into this world and which are reinforced in a highly stimulating environment. Yale University and the University of Bridgeport researchers found that when White children were presented with a slow paced television program "Mr. Rogers," and then a fast paced program, "Sesame Street," the slow paced program had a more positive affect on the behavior and learning than the more "frantic" programming of "Sesame Street."

The above is extremely significant because Black children with greater verve are often bored with "Mr. Rogers" and many prefer "Sesame Street." Unfortunately, the classroom takes the pace of "Mr. Rogers" with each passing year. Black children, especially Black boys, may not be hyperactive, they simply are not White or female; and the curriculum may be too slow. I would suggest that lectures, readings, and individual tasks be shortened, and that more group projects, movement to "hands-on" learning centers be incorporated. I would hope that high school geometry teachers do not think I am only suggesting this to the primary division. If geometry, history, physics, and English teachers can't provide hands-on experiences like the military, then the lack of motivation, best expressed by poor grades, boredom and cheating will continue. I would also suggest as a mutual compromise that Black parents reduce our childrens' sugar intake and television viewing, and provide meditation exercises.

(2) Influenced more by their peer group.

First a teacher sensitive and respectful of the culture would not embarrass the child in front of such a valued group. Secondly, in one of my classes I asked the students, "How do you stay cool with your friends?" Almost all of them said by breaking the rules, and other negative behavior such as poor grades. On the same paper, I asked them about things they wanted to improve—career goals etc.—and they all invariably had high ambitions and wanted to do right. How can they individually want to do right, but collectively want to be negative? How can a child act one way by himself and be totally different in front of his friends? (That reminds me of the KKK member who so cowardly hides behind sheets and collectively beats on individuals, or teenage gangs that are afraid of one on one confrontation, but thrive on gang beatings).

I see the peer group as one of my competitors, but I also respect its influence. I do not believe we can strip the power away from the peer group. (Unless the children have strong self-esteem as well as peer esteem). I believe the best way to approach the peer group is by reprogramming, not elimination. The session is titled Unity/Criticism/Unity (U/C/U) which I describe in detail in my book *Developing Positive Images*. This session attempts, with adult direction, to let the peer group determine what is best. We have to find ways to reprogram the male peer group to believe being smart is being cool.

(3) Greater interest in math than in reading.

In a left brain oriented curriculum, subjects are taught in isolation from each other. Reading and writing, reading and science, reading and math, and art and math etc., have become separate. I first propose that a more interdisciplinary approach and an avalanche of word problems be incorporated into the math curriculum. Please remember, because of Black children's oral orientation, they should be encouraged to explain their operations at the board.

Problems in reading are a result of a movement away from phonics, the increase in television viewing, and the lack of relevant books for Black children in the classroom. A relevant curriculum would want to show the need to read before skill applications. Black children deserve books that describe their cultural experiences.

(4) More advanced skills in gross versus fine motor.

Large numbers of Black boys enter the primary division behind girls in fine motor functions. Homes that supply boys exclusively with trucks and balls do not help their sons on school projects that accentuate pencils, crayons, and scissors. Teachers should not only be aware of the double standards at home, but give boys more time in this area, without negative value judgments being placed. Black boys simply have had less exposure to fine motor skills. The statement that their maturation rate is slow is too simplistic, and does not appreciate the nature/nurture relationship. Please understand that these same clumsy boys could become excellent brain surgeons. Learning centers need to provide both skills with teachers evaluating them equally. Fill your classroom with science projects, animals, and plants.

(5) Keen interest in fine arts.

I suggested that every concept include readings, oral presentations, pictures, artifacts, and *fine arts*. Black boys often express their cognition and sensitivity through art. Black boys often learn a speech or story better through music than a book. A person who chooses to teach Black children without music or art is an instructor not a teacher. Fine arts and the oral tradition are two cornerstones of Black culture. An excellent lesson plan would be to culminate every unit with a play. Does it really matter if students express their understanding on paper, orally, with a portrait, object, or dramatically?

(6) Larger and more sensitive ego.

In a patriarchal society controlled by White men, and with very few Black male role models available, Black boys don't know how to express their male ego. Creative teachers not only must teach boys to differentiate between battles and wars, but they must find ways for this leadership ability to be expressed. This will not happen with female teachers who bring their "political baggage" mentioned earlier into the classroom. Suggestions include:

(a) Encourage boys to be the master of ceremonies.
(b) Encourage boys to be captains of learning centers and academic teams.
(c) Designate the most aggressive boys to be classroom monitors.
(d) Encourage boys to read aloud and go to the board.

(7)The oral tradition: Playing the dozens, signifying, and rappin.

In the chapter on Female Teachers and Black Male Culture, the dozens were explained. This section will look at how this "skill" can be transferred into the classroom. When I see a Black boy demonstrate the ability to play the dozens or signify, I see a person who:

(a) Has quick thinking skills.
(b) Understands rhyme.
(c) Is expanding his vocabulary.
(d) Has public speaker potential.

The above could be used in debate, language arts, poetry, spelling bees, drama etc. I would stop every game of the dozens and turn it into:

(a) A spelling bee.
(b) A debate, and I choose the topic.
(c) A word game where I say a word and we see how many other rhyming words can be given. The winner is the one who lasts the longest.

(d) A dramatic presentation.

(e) A game called "Nightline," and let them discuss issues in an investigative style.

I repeat, you cannot teach a child that you do not understand or with whom you have not bonded. I do *not accept* the dozens in my classroom, but I *understand it*. And I let them know how good they are and that *these skills* can be transferred into other areas. As a teacher who understands the culture of the students that I teach, I use their cultural strengths, not mine, to answer the question, "What kind of curriculum and pedagogy can we develop to maximize Black boys' potential"?

Chapter V

Simba (Young Lions-Swahili)

The most frequent question that I receive from men is how can they obtain more information about Simba. There has been an expressed interest in developing a national Simba office with staff, budget, and other organizational procedures. Local and national conferences on the Black male have often allocated time to analyze the Black male child. Many people want a manual or document that will show them how to develop Black boys to be men. I asked them have they read Volume I, where the first Simba assignment was to organize a group of Black men willing to prepare Black boys for manhood. The second objective was for the men to read selected literature on the Black male, and resolve their ideological differences, so that it won't be manifested to the youth. The third concern is to identify a facility, frequency of the meeting, and target age group to be served.   Many Black men have overlooked how difficult it is to organize and study together and determine the logistics.

My experience has taught me, that those programs organized prematurely around a manual, in contrast to developing a cohesive cadre do not last long. There are Simba programs around the country operating with only one brother, who is on the verge of "burning out," because he did not start methodically. I feel it is important for the men to get to know one another, and resolve ego and political issues before organizing the youth.

I am also concerned that in our desire to save Black youth, we actually spend more time talking and reading *about* them, rather than *directly working* with them. How many actual minutes do we spend working with youth in comparison to study and discussion? It is not my desire to belittle theory, but theory without practice, or an imbalance between the two is not productive. I anguish every time I speak on the second and fourth Saturday of the month because that is when my church operates our program; but it is rewarding to know, that regardless of my attendance, the adult men are committed to work directly with the youth.

The ultimate goal of Simba is to prepare them for the rites of passage. Our boys do not know when they're men, and it is the responsibility of men to teach them. If men do not fulfill this responsibility, boys will continue to define it from a physical perspective, i.e., making a baby, fights, and the consumption of drugs, alcohol, clothes and cars. Nathan and Julia note,

"Boys reach physical puberty readily enough, but it is far more difficult, in an oppressive situation, to gain social puberty. We must recognize and actualize the difference between physical and social puberty in the Black boy's development, just as there is a difference between physical potency and social potency. Indeed, blocked from the avenues to social power and position, social potency, the Black boys may too often feel impelled to overcompensate in the physical."[1]

The two fundamental issues needed to achieve our goal is a criteria for eligibility and a complementing curriculum format. Listed below are two suggested criteria.

The Orita for Black Youth by Frank Fair.[2] There are six basic requirements which are:

1. An understanding of the Black experience in America.
2. Managing the family budget.
3. Volunteering with a community organization.
4. Exploration of career and educational opportunities.
5. Understanding the full responsibilities of citizenship.
6. The study and application of Biblical scriptures.

Nathan and Julia Hare offer *The Passage*.[3] There are seven basic requirements which are:

1. The developing of a log during the transition year.
2. The awareness and understanding of self.
3. An awareness and understanding of the immediate and extended family.
4. Service to the neighborhood and community.
5. Adopt a senior citizen.
6. The exploration of educational opportunities, including higher education.
7. Developing discipline and responsibility.

Both programs mandate that the youth be involved in the preparation of the ceremony. There is a great deal of similarity between the two programs, and while there are differences concerning economics, religion, and elders, it does not preclude any Simba program from packaging those features they deem being essential for manhood. These models are just that, models, and are to be used to further inspire the cadres.

The work becomes organizing a group of men who will study together, grow into a cohesive unit, identify a facility, determine the frequency of the meeting, identify and organize the target group of youth to be serviced, and consistently provide them with a program designed purposefully to achieve the above cited criteria. There are numerous reasons why some Simba programs have not been able to fulfill their goals. One of the reasons is adult inconsistency. One desire of Simba is to match youth with a role model. The smaller the ratio between youth and adult, the greater enhancement toward achieving the goal. When adults attend irregularly; it upsets continuity; and when they dropout completely, it puts a greater burden on the coordinator. Another factor is youth inconsistentcy. This results from age, parental involvement, and other competitive alternatives. Nathan and Julia Hare proposed the age of twelve as the target age.[4] Their argument is based on psychological and social principles, tradition, and the reality that any age after this may be too late for intervention because of the peer group and a more "physical" approach to manhood. Many Simba programs service youth ages seven through nineteen. I don't disagree with the Hare's rationale, but I do understand the hesitancy some men have expressed; honoring a twelve year old with the title of *man.*

It is also unfortunate that as the age increases, parent involvement often declines. Many parents let the upper-grade youth determine their participation. I don't believe it's an accurate assessment that there is a shortage of youth programs. I believe that many parents of primary-grade children demand their attendance, and leave it optional to their older children. Simba and similar programs need the support of parents. This is significant also because of other competitive alternatives. There is a direct correlation between age, peer group, and mass-media influence. The combination of sports, music, dating, and just "hanging out" are very attractive to youth.

The above inconsistencies, both adult and youth, provide less continuity and "time on task" to fulfill the rites of passage requirements. I would recommend that, besides addressing these issues, to designate at least one man for each criteria. Often times, when the requirements are lumped together, and no one is assigned a particular area, nothing is achieved. I propose that we draw from the high school graduation requirements model, and designate that each youth will have to satisfy each man's requirement in the particular area. This concrete approach will also lend stability because, while some adults and youth will be absent, the remaining people can continue fulfilling their objectives. This procedure encompasses the view that, while we would have liked to carry a larger number into manhood, we will concentrate on those in regular attendance.

Many Simba programs have learned from the scouts, gangs, and fraternities, and have incorporated symbols, patches of achievement, tee-shirts, sweaters, jackets, and caps to heighten solidarity. While I have concerns about the overemphasis fraternities give to social activities and Greek culture, you have to be impressed with how the Omegas, in particular, over a short period of time, can create a desire so strong, that pledgers will be branded, and swear they will be a "Q" to the day they die.

I am reminded of the work of Marcus Garvey and Elijah Muhammad. These men turned "Reds" into "Malcoms" without governmental grants and doctorates in clinical psychology. They did it with hard work, knowledge of their history, and a belief in God. Nathan Hare shares that tradition with the following:

I Am a Black Man

The evidence of anthropology now suggests that I, the Black man, am the original man, the first man to walk this vast imponderable earth. I, the Black man, am an African, the exotic single quintessence of a universal blackness. I have lost, by force, my land, my language, in essence, my life. I will seize it back so help me.

Toward that end, if necessary, I will crush the corners of the earth, and this world will surely tremble, until I, the Black man, the first and original man can arm with my woman, erect among the peoples of the universe a new society, humane to its cultural core, out of which at long last will emerge, as night moves into day, the first truly human being that the world has ever known.[5]

I believe a conspiracy has been designed to destroy Black boys; Black men must develop programs like Simba, which offers an adult role model, skill development, Black culture, and a male socialization process that will lead into the "rites of passage."

Footnotes

Chapter One

1. Kunjufu, Jawanza. *Countering the Conspiracy to Destroy Black Boys.* Chicago: African American Images, 1983, p. 24.

Chapter Two

1. Patton, James. "The Black Male's Struggle for an Education" e.d. Lawrence, Gary. *Black Men.* Beverly Hills: Sage, 1981, p. 205.
2. Arnez, Nancy. "Implementation of Desegration as a Discriminating Process." *Journal of Negro Foundation*, 1978, pp. 28-45.
3. Excerpts from "The Challenge of Blackness" delivered by Lerone Bennett at the Institute of the Balck World in Atlanta, Georgia, 1972.

Chapter Three

1. United States Statistical Abstract, 1981, passim.
2. Brown, Michael. *Image of a Man.* New York: East Publications, 1976, p. 6.

Chapter Four

1. Edmonds, Ronald. "Effective Schools for the Urban Poor." *Educational Leadership*, October, 1979, pp. 16-22.
2. Excerpts from "Black Children, Their Roots, Culture, and Learning Styles," delivered by Janice Hale in Kenosha, Wisconsin, 1986.
3. Hale, Janice. *Black Children, Their Roots, Culture, and Learning Styles.* Provo: Brigham Young University Press: 1982, pp. 32-35.
4. *Culture Linquistic Approach Social Studies Manual*, Chicago: Northeastern Illinois University Center for Inner City Studies, 1974 pp. 14-15.
5. Morgan, Harry. "How Schools Fail Black Children." *Social Policy*, January–February 1980 pp. 49-54.

Chapter Five

1. Hare, Nathan and Julia. *Bringing The Black Boy to Manhood.* San Francisco: Black Think Tank, 1985, p. 20.
2. Fair, Frank. *Orita For Black Youth.* Valley Forge: Judson Press, 1977, p. 11.
3. Hare, p. 28.
4. Ibid., p. 26.
5. Ibid., p. 43.